THUMP GOES THE RABBIT
HOW ANIMALS COMMUNICATE

BY FRAN HODGKINS · ILLUSTRATED BY TAIA MORLEY

HARPER

An Imprint of HarperCollinsPublishers

Special thanks to Dr. Fred Wasserman, Associate Professor of Biology
at Boston University, for his valuable assistance.

The Let's-Read-and-Find-Out Science book series was originated by Dr. Franklyn M. Branley, Astronomer Emeritus and former Chairman of the American Museum of Natural History–Hayden Planetarium, and was formerly co-edited by him and Dr. Roma Gans, Professor Emeritus of Childhood Education, Teachers College, Columbia University. Text and illustrations for each of the books in the series are checked for accuracy by an expert in the relevant field. For more information about Let's-Read-and-Find-Out Science books, write to HarperCollins Children's Books, 195 Broadway, New York, NY 10007, or visit our website at www.letsreadandfindout.com.

Let's-Read-and-Find-Out Science® is a trademark of HarperCollins Publishers.

Thump Goes the Rabbit: How Animals Communicate
Text copyright © 2020 Fran Hodgkins
Illustrations by Taia Morley
Illustrations copyright © 2020 by HarperCollins Publishers

Library of Congress Control Number: 2019935784
ISBN 978-0-06-249101-5 (trade bdg.) – ISBN 978-0-06-249097-1 (pbk.)
The artist used watercolor and traditional media with Adobe Photoshop to create the digital illustrations for this book.
Typography by Honee Jang
19 20 21 22 23 SPC 10 9 8 7 6 5 4 3 2 1

First Edition

To Tom—F.H.
For Maria Antonia, "you just gotta have fun."—T.M.

Birds sing. Cows moo. Dogs bark. Horses neigh. Animals use their voices a lot when they need to **communicate**.

But animals don't communicate only with their voices. Animals' ears, tails, feet, and bodies help them communicate, too. They can express everything from fear and anger to curiosity. Animals have a lot of ways to get their messages across.

The cat goes **RUB**.

Cats have special body parts called **glands** on their heads and sides. When a cat rubs up against something, the glands leave a scent behind. When other cats smell the scent, they get the cat's message: "This is where I am, and you're in my **territory**."

The rabbit goes **THUMP.**

Rabbits have long, strong back legs that are great for running fast and jumping high. They're also great for sending messages. The rabbit uses its strong legs to stomp its big back feet onto the ground. The stomp makes the ground vibrate. Other rabbits feel the **vibration**. The thump warns them, "Look out!"

The deer goes **FLASH**.

Deer are always alert for danger. If a deer is frightened, it will raise its tail and reveal a white patch on its hindquarters. Easy to see, the white patch tells other deer, "Run now!" It may also tell a **predator**, "Ha-ha! I see you and you can't catch me."

The firefly goes **FLICKER**.

On summer nights, ghostly lights flicker, some in the grass and some in the air. These flickering lights are fireflies. The males fly above the females, which are in the grass. They flash their lights to say, "Let's meet!"

The skunk goes **STOMP.**

A skunk's bold stripes act as a warning sign to other animals. But if those aren't enough, a skunk will stomp its front feet. The stomping says, "Better listen: This is your last chance before I spray!"

The fox goes **ROLL.**

When one fox meets another, sometimes they fight. But fighting is dangerous. So to avoid getting hurt, one fox may roll onto its back. When a fox shows its belly to another fox, it says, "I get it: You're in charge."

The rattlesnake goes **RATTLE.**

When it feels threatened, the rattlesnake
shakes the end of its tail. On the end are special
rings made of **keratin** (the same stuff that makes
up our fingernails). The rings make a dry clatter
that warns, "Go away, or I'll strike."

23

The whale goes **SPLASH.**

A 40-ton whale leaps out of the water and smashes back down, sending up a geyser of spray. Scientists call this behavior **breaching**. Some scientists think that a breaching whale is sometimes telling other whales, "Here I am!" But other scientists think whales breach for different reasons. Can you think of more reasons whales might breach?

The elephant goes **FLAP.**

Flap, flap, flap—elephant ears are useful for cooling off on a
hot day, but they're more than just built-in air conditioners.
They help an elephant express itself. Fast flaps mean excitement.
Flapping ears and a raised head mean, "Hello!"

The owl goes POOF.

If you are big, other animals will leave you alone. An owl fluffs out its feathers and spreads its wings when it feels threatened. Sometimes, looking big is just as good as being big.

The bee goes **WAGGLE.**

A bee waggles for a very important reason: to tell other bees it has found food. Its waggling dance tells other bees which way and how far off the food is. This way, many bees can help bring back food that would be too much for one bee to carry.

The dog goes **wag.**

A dog's tail can tell a lot. When the tail is tucked between the dog's legs, the dog is frightened. When the tail is low and wagging a little, the dog is worried. But when a dog holds its tail high and wags it fast, that's an excited dog!

Furred, finned, or feathered, animals have many ways to communicate. How do animals communicate with you?

33

BE A CITIZEN SCIENTIST: MAKE OBSERVATIONS

You can make observations just like a scientist does. All you need is patience. Sit quietly near an animal. It could be outside, where you can watch birds at a feeder, or indoors, where you can watch your pet dog or cat. (Your pet might try to get you to play at first, but if you keep sitting still, your pet will go back to what it was doing.) Watch.

What does the animal do? When does it do it?
You can write down what you see.

Your observations will help you understand animals.

1. A car drives by.

2. Sasha raises her head.

3. Her ears go forward.

4. She listens.

5. She puts her head down.

GLOSSARY

Breaching: jumping out of the water and splashing back down

Communicate: to use words or movements to express feelings or give information

Glands: body parts that make a scent the body uses or gives off

Keratin: a flexible material that makes up hair and fingernails

Predator: an animal that hunts other animals

Territory: the area where an animal lives

Vibration: a fast back-and-forth movement

COMMUNICATION

LOOK OUT! =  =

LEAVE ME ALONE! =  =

HELLO! =  =

Be sure to look for all of these books in the Let's-Read-and-Find-Out Science series:

 LEVEL 1

The Human Body:
How Many Teeth?
I'm Growing!
My Feet
My Five Senses
My Hands
Sleep Is for Everyone
What's for Lunch?

Plants and Animals:
Animals in Winter
The Arctic Fox's Journey
Baby Whales Drink Milk
Big Tracks, Little Tracks
Bugs Are Insects
Dinosaurs Big and Small
Ducks Don't Get Wet
Fireflies in the Night
From Caterpillar to Butterfly
From Seed to Pumpkin
From Tadpole to Frog
How Animal Babies Stay Safe
How a Seed Grows
A Nest Full of Eggs
Starfish
Super Marsupials
A Tree Is a Plant
What Lives in a Shell?
What's Alive?
What's It Like to Be a Fish?
Where Are the Night Animals?
Where Do Chicks Come From?

The World Around Us:
Air Is All Around You
The Big Dipper
Clouds
Is There Life in Outer Space?
Pop!
Snow Is Falling
Sounds All Around
The Sun and the Moon
What Makes a Shadow?

 LEVEL 2

The Human Body:
A Drop of Blood
Germs Make Me Sick!
Hear Your Heart
The Skeleton Inside You
What Happens to a Hamburger?
Why I Sneeze, Shiver, Hiccup, and Yawn
Your Skin and Mine

Plants and Animals:
Almost Gone
Ant Cities
Be a Friend to Trees
Chirping Crickets
Corn Is Maize
Dolphin Talk
Honey in a Hive
How Do Apples Grow?
How Do Birds Find Their Way?
Life in a Coral Reef
Look Out for Turtles!
Milk from Cow to Carton
An Octopus Is Amazing
Penguin Chick
Sharks Have Six Senses
Snakes Are Hunters
Spinning Spiders
What Color Is Camouflage?
Who Eats What?
Who Lives in an Alligator Hole?
Why Do Leaves Change Color?
Why Frogs Are Wet
Wiggling Worms at Work
Zipping, Zapping, Zooming Bats

Dinosaurs:
Did Dinosaurs Have Feathers?
Digging Up Dinosaurs
Dinosaur Bones
Dinosaur Tracks
Dinosaurs Are Different
Fossils Tell of Long Ago
My Visit to the Dinosaurs
Pinocchio Rex and Other Tyrannosaurs
What Happened to the Dinosaurs?
Where Did Dinosaurs Come From?

Space:
Floating in Space
The International Space Station
Mission to Mars
The Moon Seems to Change
The Planets in Our Solar System
The Sky Is Full of Stars
The Sun
What Makes Day and Night
What the Moon Is Like

Weather and the Seasons:
Down Comes the Rain
Droughts
Feel the Wind
Flash, Crash, Rumble, and Roll
Hurricane Watch
Sunshine Makes the Seasons
Tornado Alert
What Makes a Blizzard?
What Will the Weather Be?

Our Earth:
Archaeologists Dig for Clues
Earthquakes
Flood Warning
Follow the Water from Brook to Ocean
How Deep Is the Ocean?
How Mountains Are Made
In the Rainforest
Let's Go Rock Collecting
Oil Spill!
Volcanoes
What Happens to Our Trash?
What's So Bad About Gasoline?
Where Do Polar Bears Live?
Why Are the Ice Caps Melting?
You're Aboard Spaceship Earth

The World Around Us:
Day Light, Night Light
Energy Makes Things Happen
Forces Make Things Move
Gravity Is a Mystery
How a City Works
How People Learned to Fly
How to Talk to Your Computer
Light Is All Around Us
Phones Keep Us Connected
Running on Sunshine
Simple Machines
Switch On, Switch Off
What Is the World Made Of?
What Makes a Magnet?
Where Does the Garbage Go?